"We owe Mike Klein a debt of gratitude his putting the social media evangelists Instead of their glib advice, Mike offers separate an 'audience' into its credible tribal parts and associated mutual interests. His book is the best thing I've seen on how to understand how real people communicate in real organisations."

ROGER D'APRIX, SENIOR VICE PRESIDENT — ROI COMMUNICATION

"In one clear, cogent and deeply insightful guide, Mike Klein has set out the keys to effective communication for change. Drawing on both the past and present to help leaders create the future, the advice in this book is some of the most accurate and useful you are likely to find."

MAURY PEIPERL, PROFESSOR OF LEADERSHIP AND STRATEGIC CHANGE — IMD BUSINESS SCHOOL, AND AUTHOR OF **MANAGING CHANGE: CASES AND CONCEPTS**

"Mike Klein's distinction between social media and social communication is a vital one, and it points to where the true value of social media lies in helping to identify and mobilise the tribal forces that have always existed within organisations. A must-read for anyone involved in communicating strategy."

DR GEORG KOLB, BUSINESS DIRECTOR — DIREKTZU/STRAIGHTTO

"Mike has taken a bold step in not only challenging old-school models of corporate communication, but also the vacant bluster of social media 'gurus'. This book will provide huge help to the many people who may talk about this stuff in the pub or with colleagues, but who struggle to articulate it when it comes to putting pen to paper."

EB BANFUL, DIRECTOR — NEW BRAND TRIBALISM

"Be warned, this book might just change the way you look at social media. Drawing on his extensive experience, Mike Klein removes the hype and offers some very lucid, pertinent and effective strategies to improve its use in organisational communication."

JOÃO BAPTISTA, ASSISTANT PROFESSOR OF INFORMATION SYSTEMS — WARWICK BUSINESS SCHOOL

"In this excellent book on how to use social networks to improve communication and performance in organisations, Mike Klein shines the spotlight on 'social'. Providing great insights into how to cut through information clutter and make real connections with those who can make a difference, this is a persuasive and practical call to action."

LIZ GUTHRIDGE, MANAGING CONSULTANT — CONNECT CONSULTING GROUP, AND CREATOR OF LEAN COMMUNICATIONS

"Mike Klein goes tribal in this cogent and compelling guide, providing a valuable reminder that, when it comes to social media, it's the word 'social' that matters. In so doing, he detonates a bomb, not only under the world of top-down, one-size-fits-all communications, but also the brainless adoption of social media tools as just another channel for broadcasting them."

DAVID ZINGER, FOUNDER — EMPLOYEE ENGAGEMENT NETWORK

"Do you favour the sniper's rifle or the scattergun? Mike Klein will straighten you out with this no-nonsense, beautifully written guide to social communication. Mike's unique approach blends sociology, anthropology, front-line experience and, above all, common sense to help you improve your aim."

JON WEEDON, INTERNAL COMMUNICATION MANAGER — POKERSTARS

"'The science, art and strategy behind generating word of mouth.' That's the best definition of social communication I've ever read and, in just 80-odd pages, Mike Klein brings it to life and makes it totally actionable."

CARSTEN ROSSI, MANAGING DIRECTOR — KUHN, KAMMANN & KUHN

"Mike Klein has written a fascinating guide for navigating our increasingly social web of relationships using the communication principles used by Abraham Lincoln in the 1840s: identify your tribes, win their trust, then organise and energise them to act on your behalf. If you hate adding 'media' after 'social', you'll love Mike's approach to social communication."

GAURAV MISHRA, DIRECTOR, DIGITAL AND SOCIAL MEDIA — MSLGROUP ASIA

"What we have here is pure audacity. In this book, Klein proposes that what's missing from modern internal communication can be found in a 150-year-old political strategy. And he's right! Effective communication efforts still require strong leadership, word-of-mouth messaging, and the ability to coordinate actions that drive change. This is true regardless of whether they emphasize social or traditional media."

BETH GLEBA, BOARD MEMBER — COUNCIL FOR COMMUNICATION MANAGEMENT

"Mike provides a quick and actionable guide to why communication strategy has nothing to do with technology and everything to do with old-fashioned connection, resonance and credibility. He's taken the newest trends and grounded them in solid, proven, strategic thinking."

ALEJANDRO FORMANCHUK, PRESIDENT — ARGENTINEAN ASSOCIATION OF INTERNAL COMMUNICATION, AND AUTHOR OF **INTERNAL COMMUNICATION 2.0: A CULTURAL CHALLENGE**

FROM LINCOLN TO LINKEDIN

THE 55-MINUTE GUIDE TO
SOCIAL COMMUNICATION
BY **MIKE KLEIN**

FIRST PUBLISHED IN 2010 BY

VERB PUBLISHING LTD
THE COW SHED, HYDE HALL FARM,
BUCKLAND, HERTS SG9 0RU
UNITED KINGDOM

ISBN 978-0-9564672-2-5

TO THE COMMSCRUM TEAM FOR THEIR GUTS, COMMITMENT AND OFTEN BITING SENSES OF HUMOR. TO MY DAD FOR TEACHING ME EVERYTHING I KNOW ABOUT WRITING. AND TO MARK ABERNATHY FOR TEACHING ME THE LINCOLN RULES.

WHAT'S INSIDE

On every facing page you'll find a summary of core thoughts and ideas. Try adding them to presentations or the bottom of your emails and see if you can start a conversation.

1. INTRODUCTION

WHAT THIS BOOK'S ABOUT

This book is about how to apply strategic communication principles such as targeting, list management, and source credibility in a way that adds a social and dynamic dimension to corporate communication.

It's also a CALL TO ARMS — to seize the opportunity to kick out a failed, dictatorial, and counter-productive approach to organisational communication; equally, to block its replacement with an approach built around brainless anarchy.

For many years, organisations have generally insisted on centralised, top-down, one-size-fits-all messaging, packaged in corporate colours and delivered through mechanical and "idiot-proof" processes. Now, with the advent of a variety of online communication tools known collectively as SOCIAL MEDIA, a different call is heard — a call to surrender to the free-flowing, energetic anarchy of the online world, and to shift away from delivering messages towards facilitating them.

But Billy Joel said it best: "The good old days weren't always good, and tomorrow ain't as bad as it seems."

Social communication is the science, art and strategy behind generating word of mouth, based on deep understanding of the real social networks at play within organisations.

For starters, SOCIAL COMMUNICATION – the informal communication that intelligent use of social media can support and enable – has actually been around longer than Twitter and, indeed, longer than top-down cascades and purified corporate spin. It's what people commonly call WORD OF MOUTH. But it's not something that has to happen as if by magic, or by throwing ideas into social media forums and hoping they somehow "go viral".

Instead, social communication is the SCIENCE, ART AND STRATEGY behind generating word of mouth, built on an understanding of how and why people communicate with each other. It may not be magic, but using and mastering its advantages does require work, and giving up some classic (but now outmoded) ideas about communication. It requires an understanding of individuals and the TRIBES they take part in that drive communication in organisations or markets. And it requires a rejection of "audiences" and the tyrannical notion that communication should treat all audience members as equal, particularly through the rote transmission of top-down cascades.

Rather than focus on generic (and often irrelevant) external social networks like Facebook and Twitter, social communication focuses on the REAL SOCIAL NETWORKS already at play within organisations and communities, and on those that can be created to support new initiatives and agendas.

By connecting strategic intent with natural communication processes, social communication offers unprecedented opportunities to win.

It starts with learning how those networks form and identifying the key individuals that connect them to the broader whole. Once these real social networks are identified and understood, it then becomes possible to identify and use the most appropriate tools (social media, enhanced intranets, traditional media, face-to-face, or highly targeted communication activities) to achieve the desired outcomes.

Fundamentally, corporate communication is about setting objectives and building the relationships, coalitions and momentum to achieve them. A social communication approach offers UNPRECEDENTED FREEDOM both from the tyranny of the cascade and anarchy of an unhinged approach to social media. More importantly, by connecting strategic intent with natural communication processes, it offers UNPRECEDENTED OPPORTUNITIES TO WIN. And which would you rather do – cascade, facilitate, or win?

WHO THIS BOOK IS FOR

→   CORPORATE COMMUNICATORS – This book is for you if you are looking for a strategic edge, a more effective and efficient approach to communication, or are thinking about what social media and social communication may mean to you.

An understanding of social communication offers leaders a huge advantage – maximising support whilst minimising irritation.

→ CHANGE LEADERS – This book is for you if you are looking for an approach to communication that is tailored to maximise support and minimise resistance, thus increasing velocity while taking best advantage of internally and externally available tools.

→ CHIEF EXECUTIVES AND OTHER SENIOR MANAGERS – This book is for you if you are looking for an approach to organisational communication that generates and builds on existing sources of credibility and activity, mobilising performance rather than Dilbert-esque levels of cynicism.

→ SOCIAL MEDIA "EXPERTS" – This book is for you if you have customers seeking to drive objectives or change inside organisations, or within other bounded communities or markets, by building the necessary social communication structures from within. This avoids the unnecessary and often hostile exposure involved with doing internal campaigning on external media.

People have an inevitable attraction to the nearest and newest toy that will make life interesting, fun, and (of course) sexy.

2. IT'S NOT ABOUT SOCIAL MEDIA

"Media. Media! It's all about Media!" So said Hank, with whom I worked on a number of campaigns in my first career as a political campaign strategist and manager. Of course, Hank was a media consultant whose job was to get our campaigns to spend money on advertising, for which he would receive a not-insignificant percentage.

Even stripping away the profit motive, media have always been sexy. Whether it's television ads harsh enough to make a hapless Congressman decide not to move back home after his defeat, or free websites, Twitter accounts and pages on Facebook, people are attracted to the nearest and newest toy that will make life interesting, fun, and (of course) sexy.

The response of some in the corporate communications industry has been to leap into the market with dozens of conferences and articles on how to use social media tools. They've released tons of needless CO_2 with blather like "Social media are inevitable – you have to get on board now" or "In five years' time, communication managers will be replaced by buzz managers", or my all-time favorite "The smartest thing to do is just to jump in".

The smartest thing to do is jump in? Wow! That's like telling a pedestrian that the fastest way across the street is to

There's no such thing as "social media strategy". If it's about media, then it ain't strategy. It's tactical at best.

just jump in. Especially when the pedestrian is blind; when she has no cane; and when the intersection is in Bogota!

That's not a strategy, it's a SUICIDE MISSION!

Some practitioners are charging thousands of dollars, euros, pounds and pesos offering training in social media "strategy". But if it's about social media, IT AIN'T STRATEGY. It's tactical at best, and mostly it's a lot of oohing and aahing at voluptuous graphics and watching traffic numbers oscillate. Let's be clear...

→   SOCIAL COMMUNICATION IS NOT ABOUT SOCIAL MEDIA.

It's about understanding the SOCIAL LANDSCAPE – one populated by groups or tribes of people. It's about understanding how they connect in practical, ideological and commercial terms; how your objectives line up with theirs; and choosing the appropriate channels and technologies to identify, connect and mobilise them to achieve your success.

→   SOCIAL COMMUNICATION IS MEDIA AGNOSTIC.

It's based on TIMELESS STRATEGIC PRINCIPLES and doesn't require the addition of any new social media technologies (although it can put them to excellent use). At the same time, one can manage a social communication programme using just a phone, email, and an Excel spreadsheet.

Social communication is the communication strategy you've always wanted to do: building reciprocal connections based on two-way and multi-directional trust.

→ SOCIAL COMMUNICATION IS THE COMMUNICATION STRATEGY YOU'VE ALWAYS WANTED TO DO.

Social communication isn't about hiding behind top-down cascades and spokespeople with posh accents and Black Amex cards. It's about taking inventory of your assets and giving it your best shot — DIRECTLY, HONESTLY, POWERFULLY.

It electrifies traditional communication strategies and tools by making them more relevant and resonant to the people and groups whose support you need to succeed. It probes one's organisational and commercial life to find out who talks with whom about what, and connects with what people really care about.

It builds reciprocal connections based on TWO-WAY AND MULTI-DIRECTIONAL TRUST that go beyond one-way intent. And it allows you to avoid alienating bystanders with messages that are irritating and irrelevant.

→ SOCIAL COMMUNICATION AVOIDS SOCIAL MEDIA TRAIN WRECKS.

Social communication allows controversies to be addressed by credible allies from multiple angles, rather than being at the mercy of social media anarchy. The odds of being overtaken by events or needing to retreat behind the clipped words of a corporate spokesman are thus reduced dramatically.

Social media isn't new.

Social communication isn't new, either.

3. WHAT IS SOCIAL COMMUNICATION?

Social communication is the intelligent, strategic alternative to playing in Bogota traffic. In aggregate, it's an approach to corporate communication that integrates:

→   Formal organisational structures
→   Informal tribes in and around the organisation
→   The range of formal and informal communication media, technologies, forums and practices available.

SOCIAL COMMUNICATION ISN'T NEW

SOCIAL MEDIA ISN'T NEW. It's all just an electrified version of word of mouth – connected and accelerated with technologies and platforms that often have very short life spans.

SOCIAL COMMUNICATION ISN'T NEW EITHER. It has emerged from the basic distinctions of political campaign management and communication, such as those that emerged in the early days of American democracy, dating back to earlier permutations of democracy and governance. It also covers ideas like COMMUNI-TIES OF INTEREST that often straddle the lines between internal and external communication.

IF YOU THINK SOCIAL COMMUNICATION IS NEW, THEN THINK AGAIN. AS WE'RE ABOUT TO FIND OUT, THE SCIENCE, ART AND STRATEGY BEHIND GENERATING WORD OF MOUTH IS BEST ILLUSTRATED BY ABRAHAM LINCOLN'S PRINCIPLES FOR WINNING ELECTORAL CAMPAIGNS BACK IN 1840.

Even in a faster moving age than 1840, fundamental democratic drivers of persuasion, engagement and mobilisation remain unchanged.

ABRAHAM LINCOLN: MASTER OF SOCIAL COMMUNICATION

Before wading into the wacky wealm of web toys (apologies to Elmer Fudd), let's turn the clock back to 1840, back to a then-rural American state named Illinois. Illinois, like its confreres in the United States, had a fairly rollicking democracy back in those days – an era well pre-dating 30-second television ads, punch card ballots, campaign finance laws and automated telephone banks. (Think of it being like today, except without electricity.)

Winning in politics in 1840 was a function of two overriding factors – the quality of one's candidate and the effectiveness of the effort to manage and channel word of mouth (the original social media) to persuade and turn out voters. Emblematically, Abraham Lincoln, then an Illinois State Legislator, gave a speech on the floor of the legislature, spelling out his principles for winning electoral campaigns.

→   In each location, CREATE A SUB-COMMITTEE

→   Prepare a PERFECT LIST of all the voters

→   DETERMINE WITH CERTAINTY whom each voter will support

→   To persuade the undecideds, send in someone THEY TRUST

→   TURN OUT THE GOOD WHIGS on Election Day.

The single most important foundation of a social communication approach is the idea of a bounded universe.

Even in a faster moving age than 1840, fundamental democratic drivers of persuasion, engagement and mobilisation remain unchanged. While business communication has long considered democracy as the equivalent of anarchy, the very real anarchy of UNSTRATEGIC social media now makes these drivers acceptable for consideration and deployment within mainstream organisational communication settings.

Adapting the Lincoln Rules for organisational communication in the social media age requires, however, a reordering of the rules, leading off with the PERFECT LIST.

THE PERFECT LIST AND THE BOUNDED UNIVERSE

The single most important foundation of a social communication approach is the idea of a BOUNDED UNIVERSE – i.e. that one's audience, constituency, organisation or market consists of a finite group of people with whom you can communicate directly. In other words, you have to be able to make a list, and you have to be able to reach the people on the list (or, at the very least, the influential people on the list) – directly if possible.

This runs counter to a lot of social media blather exhorting communicators to accept that audience universes are open and unbounded. Except for the most-popular consumer goods and services, it is possible to make a useable

Except for the most popular consumer goods and services, it's possible to make a useable list of the "voters" in any market, community or organisation.

list of the "voters," or, at the very least, the opinion leaders in any market, community or organisation.

The Lincoln Rules are intriguingly spare in their definitions, and no case is more ambiguous than that of the PERFECT LIST. Such ambiguity can be liberating. The list may:

→ Include all employees, or all members of a certain formal subset (e.g. "The Top 250")
→ Include 100% of the individuals impacted by a situation or change
→ Include all of the key stakeholders involved in a critical issue or decision
→ Be simply the best attempt to find a big enough cross-section of people to launch and support an internal or external communication initiative.

INVERSION OF TRUST AND COMMUNICATION CATASTROPHES

The Lincoln Rule that is most ignored in corporate communication is the idea of SENDING IN SOMEONE THE UNDECIDEDS TRUST TO PERSUADE THE UNDECIDEDS. Almost invariably, corporations send someone the corporation (not the sceptical audience) trusts to deliver such messages, often with catastrophic effect.

Almost invariably, corporations send someone whom the corporation trusts to deliver messages to sceptical audiences, often with catastrophic effect.

Nowhere is this more apparent than in corporate internal communication. Indeed, one can make a legitimate claim that the failure to identify and leverage sources of REAL CREDIBILITY results in the majority, if not the entirety, of internal communication disasters.

Top-Down-One-Size-Fits-All (TDOSFA) communication, like cascades and traditional newsletters, retains considerable appeal for "simplicity" (read: oversimplification or dumbing down), "consistency" (read: inflexibility compounded by inconsistent delivery tone and speed) and "efficiency" (read: by delivering the same messages across the organisation, even to those unaffected).

Consider how the same exact messages could elicit a completely different response if delivered through sources trusted by those ON THE RECEIVING END instead of those doing the cascading.

The point is that the most trusted source in a given situation might not be the line manager or the CEO, and certainly isn't the disembodied corporate "we". Trust doesn't necessarily follow the boxes and lines of the organisational chart or the formal structures of a policy area or marketplace. It combines the formal and informal tribal relationships that emerge over time. Identifying and understanding these tribes, the intensity and spread of relationships they involve, and how to best connect to them, is the key to successful social communication. (MORE ON THIS LATER.)

Audiences are weaker than tribes in organisations for one main reason – they lack the core ingredient of SELF-IDENTIFICATION.

DETERMINING WITH CERTAINTY

The second biggest cause of corporate communication disasters is for the organisation to assume that because it holds an opinion, it can command the agreement of all who hear it.

Again this is most prevalent in the area of internal communication, because in many countries (most notably the United States) employers consider employees to be their property – to be told not only how to ACT, but also how to THINK while on the job.

Naturally, this presents a challenge to the necessary process of identifying allies, opponents and undecideds. In an environment where resistance is not officially recognised, it requires some creativity to measure and address it honestly.

That's not a total barrier to developing a viable list of supporters – the best first step towards Lincoln's point of DETERMINING WITH CERTAINTY. It simply requires an effort to rate those supporters' enthusiasm levels numerically, perhaps leaving room for skeptics and resisters lower on the numerical scale (e.g. a simple 5-point rating system, where 3 = basic or pro-forma support, 4 = enthusiasm, and 5 = a willingness to volunteer pro-actively on key activities).

Where there is appetite and access, there are easier tools to use, such as online surveys, desk research conducted through

Inner networks are the arms, legs, eyes and ears of a network communication strategy, bridging the gap between the lines and boxes of the org chart and the conversations of the real organisation.

internal directories, and particularly sites like LinkedIn. These are often an excellent starting point for a successful list and map-building exercise. Best of all is the intelligence gathered face-to-face and over the phone through one's inner and extended communication networks within the organisation.

CREATING YOUR INNER NETWORK

Once you have a working version of your PERFECT LIST, and you have some idea of the support or enthusiasm level of a cross- section of participants, it becomes time to recruit and mobilise an inner network, which lines up with Lincoln's exhortation to "have a subcommittee in every district". This inner network would initially align tightly with the organisation chart and fulfills the roles of:

→   Providing an informal means of communicating that aligns with the formal structures of the organisation
→   Allowing for broad, yet subtle, information gathering from other parts of the organisation
→   Assisting in validating and checking local impact of formal or informal communication initiatives
→   Helping collect and validate information about informal and tribal constituencies in their areas
→   Helping collect and validate information about informal leaders within their local contexts.

At its core, social communication is built around tribes and networks that are constantly forming and reforming around the organisation.

Essentially, the inner network is parallel to the main informal communication network and serves as a first port of call for intelligence gathering about local tribal landscapes.

It can help manage the logistics involved in distribution and information flow between you, the larger informal network, and the formal network as it exists on the organisation chart. This also alleviates much of the hassle normally involved in internal communication – a major benefit when the initial objections about any change in internal communication approaches tend to focus on resources and maintenance.

TRIBES AND NETWORKS

At its core, social communication is based on:

→   Identifying the relevant informal groups within an organisation or community

→   Eliciting their relevant values, stories, language, structures, heroes and relative importance to their members

→   Identifying key leaders, influencers, hubs (those who connect lots of people within a tribe) and bridges (those who act as connectors/facilitators between multiple tribes)

Rating the commitment level of participants adds considerable depth to an understanding of an organisation's social dynamics.

→ Building a list or database of individuals with their formal and tribal affiliations (and, where possible, rating their intensities of affiliation)

→ Using that database as a powerful, dynamic tool to drive messaging, build coalitions and tribes of your own, and collect information with pinpoint effectiveness.

Popular terms which cover this realm include NETWORKED COMMUNICATION (treating groupings as informal or "hidden" networks) and TRIBAL COMMUNICATION (focusing on the nature, power, spread and cohesion of these groups, particularly as they transcend the limitations of the organisation chart).

Identifying and analysing tribes, their dynamics and structures is by far the biggest part of a social communication effort and will be the focus of its own section, which follows this overview.

TURNING OUT THE GOOD WHIGS

Back in 1840, Abraham Lincoln was a member of a political party called the Whigs. As the term Whig has little popular meaning, it makes excellent shorthand for one's own allies and supporters.

Rather than getting people to advocate decisions they haven't bought into, inclusion is far more effective when used to get them on board BEFORE decisions are made.

When Lincoln said, "Turn out the Good Whigs," he didn't mean, "Wake up everyone indiscriminately and make everyone vote, especially the people who hate us." He meant, "Make sure all the people who are genuinely on our side do what we need them to do."

Corporate presumptiveness often exacerbates difficult situations because it unwittingly arouses and mobilises resistance as well as assistance. Sometimes this is done blindly. Other times this is done in the name of "inclusion" or "fairness". This ignores the fact that inclusion is far more effective when used to get people on board BEFORE decisions are made – not after.

At its core, a social communication approach combines efficiency and effectiveness by focusing on mobilising and engaging those whose help is genuinely critical.

How does one find these people?

Yep: at some point, THEY'LL BE ON THE PERFECT LIST.

A tribe is any informal, but identifiable, grouping of people that exists within an organisation, market or community, representing their main form of "diversity".

4. TRIBES: COMMUNITIES OF INTEREST AND NETWORKS OF TRUST

The term "tribe" is very much in vogue at the moment, with numerous thinkers like SETH GODIN and DAVE LOGAN penning books on how to build them and lead them (books I recommend highly, by the way).

But while they discuss tribes mainly in the context of the outcomes they seek, or the attitudes they share, there's also a broader view – that of a tribe as ANY INFORMAL, BUT IDENTIFIABLE, GROUPING OF PEOPLE that exists within an organisation, market or community. (They are distinct from "teams", which are formal organisational groups under the authority of line managers.)

Tribes are what add colour to organisational and community life. Indeed, they form the main form of "diversity" which exist within organisations (either to the chagrin or satisfaction of HR departments).

Tribes often define how people identify themselves. They can range in significance from shared allegiance to a soft drink to shared belief in a theology. They can be incubated solely within a corporation or community, or can unite people within the corporation or community on the basis of external interests or affiliations.

Forget the multicoloured team picture. Real diversity in an organisation is a function of the vibrancy of its informal tribes.

Imagine this...

A company which normally mandates the wearing of navy blue suits has a "choose your clothes" day, with one stipulation – you must wear at least two things that symbolise the most important things in your life.

The day comes, and the place is a revelation. Some employees are wearing football shirts, others from their nations of origin and still others from their respective universities. Others are wearing items of religious significance – crucifixes or headscarves, for example. Brooches with children's and pet's pictures are in evidence, along with a few wrinkled t-shirts bearing the picture of Tux the Penguin (mascot of Linux programmers everywhere).

THE HEART OF DIVERSITY

Real diversity in any organisation is a function of the VIBRANCY OF ITS INFORMAL TRIBES. In a way, this is blindingly obvious. As organisations seek to augment the numbers of members of under-represented groups and incorporate different perspectives, their efforts strengthen the internal tribes comprising members of those groups. Once aboard, new employees will seek out tribes with which to build their own networks for growth and protection, or create their own.

Groups who form tribes outside organisations will also form tribes inside them, so long as members can find each other.

Moreover, new recruits from ethnic minorities tend to have a broader range of tribal contacts than might be expected. Indeed, ethnic minority hires often become prized social communication connections, as they tend become engaged members of multiple networks.

Even when the marketing folks take over from HR – this time seeking to drive individuals to produce relentlessly consistent customer experiences – they too find there is no way to suppress the natural human drive to affiliate with like-minded folks. Indeed, tribes can and do form along a broad diversity of lines, the most common including:

→   LENGTH OF SERVICE. A common dividing line is between "lifers" and "new hires" – two tribes that often display sharply different attitudes to change, and very different dynamics. New hires often display greater objectivity and clarity about what needs to change within a unit, but "lifers" know each other far better, making them more cohesive. This is not to say all "lifers" are created equal. Indeed, while new hires tend to share many views about their new organisation and its culture and be open to change, lifers tend to break into two groups – "defenders" (who want things to stay the way they are), and "changers" (who want to leave the business

Tribes emerge in a number of ways. They can morph out of teams, or they can reflect prior affiliations, current interests, or common origins.

in better shape than they found it in). But it takes some degree of intention to fuse the "lifer-changers" with the new hires in a change context.

→ LANGUAGE. Language in the workplace can be a major tribe former, particularly in its ability to reinforce national and cultural ties and facilitate private conversations in otherwise open settings.

→ EDUCATIONAL LEVEL/DEGREE OF STUDY/SCHOOL ATTENDED. Alumni ties and academic backgrounds produce tribal ties that easily run across team lines, as it is generally easy to identify fellow graduates or profession members when one joins an organisation. Equally, managers who lack university qualifications may keep an eye out for fellow "school leavers" as they move up the ranks.

→ CORPORATE INDUCTION CLASSES, HIGH POTENTIAL AND CROSS-FUNCTIONAL GROUPS. Large companies may intentionally create tribes and informal networks through their education and training exercises, their selection of leadership-potential groups, and the incubation of cross-functional groups to address specific organisational issues. As HR tends to own these

Any identifiable group with three or more participants, in any community or organisation, is effectively a tribe.

processes and lists, this is a case where their support can provide access to a major organisational asset.

→ SPORTS LOYALTIES. Many sports teams have global followings far larger than their urban bases, providing grounds for affinity that transcends location and can serve as the basis for broader tribal ties.

The above list is fairly comprehensive but by no means exhaustive. Any identifiable group with three or more participants, in any community or organisation, is effectively a tribe. If they have strong bonds above and beyond their formal roles, formal teams can also be considered tribes, but for purposes of this analysis, informal tribes and networks remain the focus.

RESEARCHING TRIBES — THE CRITICAL STEP

Coming into a blue-suited organisation, most of the tribes mentioned above are unlikely to be identifiable at first glance. Merely to identify tribes requires some initial research, and further research is required to understand which tribes are situationally significant, what drives them, who their members and leaders are, and what cues or concessions will move them in a desired direction.

Conducting and compiling tribal research is an inexact science. The first step is to survey your inner network.

Compiling the research

As tribal information rarely exists as such in official organisational databases, conducting and compiling tribal research is an inexact science – one based to a substantial degree on personal investigation and iteration, and on making maximum use of a core communication network.

Indeed, that network is the best place to start – to find out what tribes each employee IN YOUR INNER NETWORK belongs to and connects with. A first step would be a survey for your inner network members that identifies the following details:

→	BASIC DEMOGRAPHICS – age, location, department, day job, where day job fits, reporting lines

→	INTERESTS – company issues, external hobbies and activities

→	AFFILIATIONS – company origin, academic backgrounds

→	CORE CONVERSATIONS – local issues, company-wide issues, specific initiatives

→	CONVERSATION PARTNERS – e.g. "Who are the people you talk with most about the company?"

Completing this survey – and integrating its inputs into the PERFECT LIST – will help orchestrate further investigation, particularly if members of the core network also belong to

There is nothing to stop you from using public sources like LinkedIn, if not specifically forbidden by law or corporate policy.
Use them well.

tribes that merit deeper investigation. The "conversation partners" question becomes the most tangible piece to form the first part of a social network map identifying relationships and connections within the group.

Desk research

Desk research should begin with LinkedIn where possible, as it allows you to identify key biographical and affiliation data about many of the people in your organisation (for example, one-third of my current organisation is present); and, where the person allows, you can actually identify and begin to map connections between key players.

At a minimum, you should add your WHOLE INNER NETWORK as contacts, and you shouldn't be afraid of using LinkedIn to introduce yourself to other key players and add them to your network.

Other resources – to integrate in with LinkedIn research wherever possible – include internal employee directories, regional networks like Xing in Central Europe, and even Facebook or Twitter (with the understanding that professional use is generally more sensitive than it is for LinkedIn).

If you can't walk around every location, members of your core network can lend a hand.

JUST BE SENSIBLE. Again, iteration is the key. While it may be unfeasible to research every employee in an organisation or a given population, it is important to do desk research, as the importance of certain individuals becomes apparent. In smaller groups, such as the teams working on change programmes, it is easier to cover the population.

Research by "walking around"

Going beyond desk research to get a sense of what is happening in the physical environment is useful too. This research can collect everything from visual cues (desk and office decorations, notice-board comments) and who is talking with whom, along with informal conversations that elicit the frequency and priority with which key terminology is used.

UNDERSTANDING TRIBAL DYNAMICS

Alongside the collection of individual data, it is also imperative to develop a good (if not exhaustive) understanding of tribal dynamics, such as whether the tribe is viable, how it works, who is involved in it and where it is most active. This becomes possible as one connects with likely or active tribe members. Key elements to be identified and explored include:

Tribes have histories, leaders and legends. Learn all you can about them.

→ TRIBE IDENTIFICATION. What is this tribe? Is the tribe viable? How does it work? Who is involved? Where is it most active? What drives affiliation to the tribe? What are the boundaries that define WHO'S IN AND WHO'S OUT? Can a membership list of some accuracy be compiled (for incorporation into, or crosschecking with the PERFECT LIST)?

→ THE TRIBE'S LIKELY IMPACT on your desired objectives or outcome – i.e. assessment based on overlap with key players, or those targeted by objective or outcome owners

→ VALUES. The principles the tribe considers important, and which guide the way it operates

→ HISTORY. Stories about the group's origins, specific events of internal importance, acts of individual notoriety within the tribe, or events marking key interactions with other parts of the organisation

→ INTERACTIONS. Certain tribes have pre-existing relationships with each other – relationships that can either be leveraged (where interrelationships are positive) or that may need to be overcome (where tribes are essentially rivals). Tribal rivalries can be based on issues of principle (wedded

Understand what holds tribes together –
it's the key if you need to pull them apart.

to different approaches, technologies or geographies) or they can be based on external social tensions. Does the tribe see itself as autonomous and proactive, or does it see itself as being at the mercy of "the organisation"?

→ TRIBAL LANGUAGE. This can range from tribe-specific technical jargon, to the way tribe members describe outsiders, to terms used by alumni of previous acquisitions. Tone plays a role as well – does the tribe see itself as autonomous and proactive, or does it see itself as being dominated by "the organisation", or of other tribal actors or individuals?

→ LEADERSHIP STRUCTURE AND STRENGTH. Even informal tribes can have startlingly formal leadership structures, particularly if they conduct ongoing activities. Others can have certain members whom they hold in particular esteem, and still others can have rival factions.

→ COHESION AND IDENTIFICATION PRINCIPLES. What ideas hold tribes together? Some tribes, such as those of ethnic or national origin, may have externally defined cohesion principles. Others may be held together by affinities or relationships (common social activities), and others around common values.

How tribes view themselves may be the most important thing you need to know.

→ FACTIONALISING PRINCIPLES. What divides tribes into sub-tribes? Some tribes are large or intense enough to have factional tensions, or (at the very least) well-held differences of opinion. For example, in a post-merger situation, they could concern the extent to which the new organisation, its values and practices should be embraced beyond the minimum requirements.

→ COLLECTIVE SELF-IMAGE. Dealt with in much more detail in DAVE LOGAN's book, TRIBAL LEADERSHIP, collective self-image issues range from victimhood ("We don't get listened to") to defiance ("Without us, they're cooked!") to intense self-confidence ("We're the baddest dudes in the house!").

→ COMMUNICATION MECHANISMS AND FLOWS WITHIN TRIBES. Depending on size, role and geographic dispersion, communication flows within tribes vary dramatically. Some rely on in-person gatherings, while others may be connected through a seemingly random flow of individual and group emails.

→ SUPPORT FOR ORGANISATIONAL INITIATIVES. Where known or visible, tribes (and their members) should be assessed for their support, indifference or opposition to organisational

Sometimes you have to just dive in and investigate.

initiatives, or at the very least for their intensity of observable support for each initiative.

PERSONAL EXPLORATION

Sometimes, learning about tribal dynamics – particularly at the front end of a change programme – requires personal effort to identify and build connections that will create the network you need with the available tribes.

In this case, the key is to understand one's own connections with the groups one needs to succeed. For example, to understand a Muslim tribe, I may be better off having a conversation with a Turkish colleague, whom I can regale with my knowledge of Turkish soccer and my Saturday morning dose of Mehmet Efendi coffee, than I might be with the Palestinian colleague, with whom the conversation could deteriorate into an unhealthy argument about our personal political views.

A series of lunch conversations at my new company with transplants from my former firm could, in turn, give both an understanding of how its "mafia" works in the new company, and of whom in the CURRENT ORGANISATION is likely to share common views on specific change issues.

The list and map of the bridges, hubs and experts is the distilled essence of a streamlined communication network.

MAPPING TRIBES

Mapping could either be a manual task focusing broadly on individuals identified as participating in multiple tribes and their interactions (drawing on the ability to manipulate through Excel or a database program), or a fully automated task using social network mapping software (such as Orgnet or NodeXL) that is capable of mapping all or a large part of a substantial organisation. Three key types of individuals should be identified:

→ BRIDGES – i.e. people who belong to multiple tribes
→ HUBS – i.e. leaders and influencers who are best connected within each tribe
→ EXPERTS – i.e. those with whom people within the network consult, inside and (where applicable) outside the organisation.

Indeed, the list and map of the bridges, hubs and experts is the distilled essence of a streamlined communication network – one that may be capable of absorbing and distributing information based on relevance and resonance, as well as organisational spread.

IT'S BEEN A WHILE SINCE WE FIRST MENTIONED THEM SO, AS A SUMMARY, LET'S REMIND OURSELVES HOW SOCIAL COMMUNICATION MAPS TO THE LINCOLN RULES...

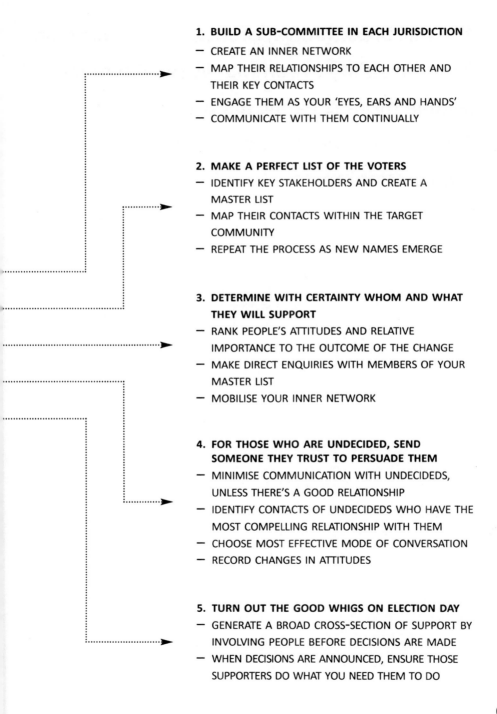

1. BUILD A SUB-COMMITTEE IN EACH JURISDICTION
- CREATE AN INNER NETWORK
- MAP THEIR RELATIONSHIPS TO EACH OTHER AND THEIR KEY CONTACTS
- ENGAGE THEM AS YOUR 'EYES, EARS AND HANDS'
- COMMUNICATE WITH THEM CONTINUALLY

2. MAKE A PERFECT LIST OF THE VOTERS
- IDENTIFY KEY STAKEHOLDERS AND CREATE A MASTER LIST
- MAP THEIR CONTACTS WITHIN THE TARGET COMMUNITY
- REPEAT THE PROCESS AS NEW NAMES EMERGE

3. DETERMINE WITH CERTAINTY WHOM AND WHAT THEY WILL SUPPORT
- RANK PEOPLE'S ATTITUDES AND RELATIVE IMPORTANCE TO THE OUTCOME OF THE CHANGE
- MAKE DIRECT ENQUIRIES WITH MEMBERS OF YOUR MASTER LIST
- MOBILISE YOUR INNER NETWORK

4. FOR THOSE WHO ARE UNDECIDED, SEND SOMEONE THEY TRUST TO PERSUADE THEM
- MINIMISE COMMUNICATION WITH UNDECIDEDS, UNLESS THERE'S A GOOD RELATIONSHIP
- IDENTIFY CONTACTS OF UNDECIDEDS WHO HAVE THE MOST COMPELLING RELATIONSHIP WITH THEM
- CHOOSE MOST EFFECTIVE MODE OF CONVERSATION
- RECORD CHANGES IN ATTITUDES

5. TURN OUT THE GOOD WHIGS ON ELECTION DAY
- GENERATE A BROAD CROSS-SECTION OF SUPPORT BY INVOLVING PEOPLE BEFORE DECISIONS ARE MADE
- WHEN DECISIONS ARE ANNOUNCED, ENSURE THOSE SUPPORTERS DO WHAT YOU NEED THEM TO DO

The real breakthrough of social communication isn't the ability to communicate with more people more cheaply. It's the ability to focus communication on the few people who matter most.

5. USING SOCIAL COMMUNICATION IN AN INTERNAL CONTEXT

Given that the process of researching, building and maintaining an understanding of one's network(s) is so intricate, the actual communication activities that deploy that network may seem really simple and obvious.

Such appearances belie the fact that the hard work and the precision targeting made available by the PERFECT LIST allow the majority of communication activities to avoid reaching those who are uninvolved or uninterested, and to make best use of those who connect with multiple individuals and multiple teams.

While a social communication approach may be criticised for being time consuming, it consumes far less overall time than forcing all employees to sift through countless irrelevant and irritating communication items. Indeed, while many people think the breakthrough of social media is the ability to communicate with larger numbers of people more cheaply, the REAL BREAKTHROUGH of social communication may well be how it improves outcomes by focusing communication on FEWER PEOPLE — those who can MAKE THE MOST DIFFERENCE.

Tribal focus helps your communication hit its target, while flying above or below the radar at the same time.

In general, there are two ways to use social communication in an organisational context.

→   SELECTIVELY DITCH OR DOWNPLAY the use of broadcast communication tools, and instead leverage your informal networks.

→   TRIBALISE BROADCAST MEDIA by injecting tribal and team imagery and language into broadly shared corporate communication.

This helps to:

→   Communicate with broadly dispersed tribes
→   Reinforce the fact that that initiatives have the support and blessing of tribal leaders
→   Sharpen the case for tribal cooperation above and beyond what is possible behind the scenes
→   Demonstrate that the organisation values the spread, depth and contributions of significant tribes
→   Reduce reliance on potentially ineffective communication channels.

Most tribes love to see their members celebrated in the broadcast media, internally or externally.

SOME TIPS TO MAKE IT WORK BETTER

→ Tribe-sensitive pronouncements or policy decisions should take the form of quotes – either from a tribal leader or from a corporate or community leader directed at a given tribe or tribes.

→ Tribal leaders should be subtly identified as a member of whichever tribes are relevant (e.g. current location, previous location, previous company, professional specialty, number of years in company).

→ Enough tribal language and jargon should be used to establish familiarity, but explained so that lay readers can understand. In other words, use THEIR IMAGES and speak THEIR LANGUAGE (not yours).

→ Blogs from the most visible positional and tribal leaders can reinforce and contextualise information, provided they are in their own voices.

Having a credible source appear in an unexpected venue or channel can offer the power of surprise and greater impact.

IDENTIFYING CREDIBLE SOURCES

Once the mapping is complete, finding credible voices to appeal within key tribes, and those with appeal across multiple tribal lines becomes the next step. Such voices should be identified along with the communication venues and tools they prefer to use.

However, these preferences should serve only as guidelines, since having a credible source appear in an unexpected venue or channel on occasion can offer the power of surprise and, therefore, greater impact.

LEVERAGING INTERNAL NETWORKS

The process for leveraging internal networks is very simple with a well-annotated spreadsheet, and really depends on the intent of particular communications – whether they seek to inform, involve or mobilise.

Informing

In a networked-communication environment, any communication that seeks to inform should reach all who need to know, without disturbing those who don't.

Social communication is about the selectivity to be effective without being offensive.

Consequently, an informational message incorporates:

→ Identifying all those who need to know
→ Identifying the people on the list who need to know
→ Identifying those key contacts who belong to the impacted teams and tribes
→ Selecting the most effective approach for delivering the message.

Involving

Beyond the basic downward push of cascade-style tactics, social communication approaches can help initiatives gain legitimacy and traction by helping to ensure that the groups most important to an issue are participating – particularly if a question is opened to broader input.

These groups can be most beneficial in ensuring that a consensus is built around an initiative at the beginning, and in demonstrating leadership flexibility in addressing concerns after initiatives are announced.

Assuming that any substantial change is portended, or any potential for controversy exists, an approach that is genuine about seeking participation from credible voices in the organisation, acting upon their contributions, and sharing the

Sometimes social communication isn't the best approach.

results of those actions is crucial (except in those rare cases where outcomes and messages must be pre-scripted and pre-ordained).

Indeed, if there is no flexibility it may well be unwise to attempt the use of social communication approaches because it can undermine their future credibility in the organisation. To help identify whom best to involve, a well-maintained PERFECT LIST would identify all the main formal and tribal ties an individual has, ensuring the ability to select individuals who each represent broad or deep networks.

On issues of high sensitivity – particularly issues for which there was limited ability to create the appearance of broad consensus early on – individuals who are seen to be broadly credible can be recruited not only to participate, but also to speak for and endorse the outcomes, thus beginning the process of securing broader acceptance.

Mobilising

Organisational mobilisation involves different groups of people doing different things at different times, often in a tightly managed sequence. A social communication approach, therefore, can be readily aligned in change management situations with programme and project management – supporting the identification

A focused mobilisation communication effort can avoid drawing undue attention from uninvolved staff.

of those who should be mobilised for each activity, and ensuring that they are on board and in place at the required time.

At the same time, a focused mobilisation communication effort can avoid drawing undue attention from uninvolved staff, for whom a constant barrage of programme jargon and milestone dates can have a numbing effect.

List selection for mobilisation can be quite sensitive. Indeed, the access to the PERFECT LIST is an asset that can bring the lead communicator into the room when the decisions about whom to involve are made, and make him/her a critical player in ensuring that the group is balanced.

Guess what? A lot of these rules apply to external use of social communications as well.

6. INTEGRATING SOCIAL COMMUNICATION WITH EXTERNAL COMMUNICATION

While much of the focus here is on the application of social communication approaches in an internal context, guess what? A lot of these rules apply to EXTERNAL USE of social communication as well. If the outcomes you are supporting involve external as well as internal actors, social communication can:

→   FORM THE BASIS OF YOUR WHOLE COMMUNICATION STRATEGY

If you have a BOUNDED UNIVERSE of actors, and know reasonably well who they are, there is nothing stopping you from using the same approaches – i.e. making a list, determining support, focusing credible persuasion and mobilising selectively.

    The only major difference is that your network research will have to go outside organisational boundaries, and that you will have to be more creative about how to identify social networks that exist in markets or other external environments.

Social communication might even take us beyond tired "living the brand" programmes and provide a context for employees to invest more of their personal credibility in the stuff you'd like them to do.

→ ALLOW YOU TO ACKNOWLEDGE AND INFLUENCE ROLE OF EMPLOYEES IN SUPPORT OF EXTERNAL OBJECTIVES.

One of the most underutilised corporate assets is the social credibility of employees. Even in consumer-oriented markets that are too big to handle entirely through social communication, social communication can effectively persuade and mobilise employees to invest their own credibility in support of the company, and can influence how employees discuss the company, its products and its activities within the larger community.

This is not just the "brand ambassadorship" advocated by "living the brand" enthusiasts, though it includes proactive representation of the brand by those to sign up to do it. It also involves the ONGOING DIALOGUES AND RELATIONSHIPS that employees have in the community (such as for supporting recruitment and reinforcing their employer's reputation), and can create a stronger context for the responsibilities employees share in putting their employers' activities in a positive light.

A few final words of guidance. Like, "Don't eat yellow snow."

7. NOW CAN I PLAY WITH SOCIAL MEDIA?

The time may have come for you to integrate your communication and social communication strategies with some social media tools. A few final words of guidance:

→ Make sure you're using the SAME TOOLS as the networks you want to communicate with. For example, don't open a Twitter account and start tweeting internal content if you have no idea who inside (or outside) the company is interested in you on Twitter.

→ Make sure your tools WORK FOR YOUR NETWORKS. Yammer, Socialcast and Jive (internal messaging services that provide easy connections and some mapping data) may be appealing, but they can be dominated by a few loud voices and might not reach certain places.

→ You can make your intranet more tribe-friendly, as there are features such as groups and boards that will provide online infrastructure. But your intranet WILL NEVER PROVIDE YOU WITH THE REAL MAP of who is talking with whom about what.

It's not about migrating stuff onto social media platforms. It's about connecting those conversations to activities where they naturally exist.

→   MAKE FRIENDS WITH THE TECHIES. Learn about your IT organisation and the people in it who might be inclined to help you with your technical requirements. Better still, see if they can give you a map of email flows, if local laws allow.

→   CONSIDER INCORPORATING SOCIAL ELEMENTS INTO TRADITIONAL TOOLS. An ability to conduct polls, rate poll questions and convene online discussions could be valuable additions to an intranet site, and perhaps more appropriate than a Facebook page in many contexts.

The main thing to remember with social communication, however, is that it's not really about trying to migrate conversations and networks and ongoing business activities onto social media platforms. It's about connecting with those conversations, networks and activities WHERE THEY NATURALLY EXIST.

It's not about social media for social media's sake. It's about doing what it takes to HELP YOUR ORGANISATION WIN. If social media can help you win, use it. If not, and you use it anyways, YOU ARE HEADED FOR A TRAIN WRECK.

The real revolution is that top-down, one-way, one-size-fits-all communication is being blown out of the water.

8. SUMMING UP

People who think the communication revolution is all about social media have failed to see WHAT'S REALLY HAPPENING. The real revolution is that the myth of top-down, one-way, one-size-fits-all communication is being BLOWN OUT OF THE WATER. Online social media are rendering the control myth untenable, because they visibly alter this top-down flow and make it easier for people to get involved without needing a huge amount of standing or external visibility. Of course, the control myth was NEVER VALID IN THE FIRST PLACE (that's why social communication isn't new). But its burial makes it possible to have a direct conversation about REAL SOCIAL COMMUNICATION with even the most conservative C-suite types.

There's a temptation to respond to C-Suite concerns by unleashing the bosses on Twitter. But the more powerful alternative is to step back and think about the INFORMAL SOCIAL AND CONVERSATIONAL NETWORKS that drive real communication – not just the tools that may help give it shape and velocity.

The stakes are high. But using the techniques and tools explored here, you now have access to an approach to communication that channels POWER, PRECISION AND PASSION directly to the challenges you and your organisation face. And by using them, you'll avoid being a SOCIAL MEDIA TRAIN WRECK.

9. SOCIAL COMMUNICATION GLOSSARY

AUDIENCE – a fictitious notion of a discrete group of people in an organisation or community that "receives" a message. (See also NETWORK).

BLATHER – nonsense, drivel, pointless conversation; the chosen dialect of the vast majority of self-proclaimed social media gurus.

BOUNDED UNIVERSE – an understanding of the finite nature of the group involved in achieving or being impacted by a given outcome, whether it is a full list of participants, a geographic boundary, or a specified division of an organisation. The domain for creating your PERFECT LIST (see below).

CASCADE – a traditional approach to organisational communication where pronouncements or presentations are issued at the corporate level, and distributed through the management hierarchy. While still a preferred tool for conveying changes in policy, their variable speed and vulnerability to manager sabotage make them a poor means of delivering messaging involving speed or emotion.

CHANGE LEADERS – managers or leaders who have accountability for the success of specific or systemic change programmes in organisations.

DEMOCRATIC – pertaining to the ability of people to choose to abstain, engage or agitate within their communities. Despite the protestation of certain corporate leaders, all organisations have at least some democratic characteristics – the ability to share and withhold, to remain or resign, and above all, to choose whom to trust and communicate with.

ELMER FUDD – American cartoon character whose ineptitude as a hunter (which contributed greatly to the longevity of his nemesis, Bugs Bunny) was exceeded only by his inability to pronounce the letter "R".

INTENT – the driving *raison d'être* and core objective of an organisation, independent of a desire to maximise profits and/or outputs. Visions, purposes and missions are all means of conveying or verbalising this.

MEDIA AGNOSTIC – an approach to strategy or tactics that is not dependent upon the use of any particular form of media, whether social or traditional.

NETWORK – a group of people in an organisation or community who are bound by a series of social interconnections, and who communicate and connect with each other through those interconnections.

PERFECT LIST – a list that identifies (to the maximum extent feasible at any time) the key players involved in achieving any desired outcome, and the data relevant to the role they may play in supporting, opposing, or resisting that outcome.

SOCIAL COMMUNICATION – the seemingly spontaneous communication that takes place between individuals and groups within organisations and communities. In fact, it can be influenced through strategies that identify the key social networks within an organisation, and what drives the behaviors of the key individuals connecting those networks.

SOCIAL LANDSCAPE – the layout and interrelationships between the social networks and formal structures that exist in organisations and communities.

SOCIAL MEDIA – a collection of tools (mostly online and of relatively recent vintage) designed to provide users with seemingly inexpensive access to broader audiences. Use of such tools to deliver inappropriate messages to indifferent or hostile audiences can raise the expense – and aggravation – involved considerably.

TRADITIONAL COMMUNICATION – the range and use of communication tools that preceded the advent of social media (e.g. newsletters, suggestion boxes, cascades, magazines), which are generally one-way in nature and expensive to produce.

TRIBE – a group or network within a community or organisation that is built around a common affiliation, objective or interest, usually crossing organisational boundaries or forming unofficial subsets within those boundaries. Individuals can belong to a potentially unlimited number of tribes.

TRUST – in the context of SOCIAL COMMUNICATION (see above), the quality of being seen as credible, either for being knowledgeable, or as having benign or positive motives.

WORD OF MOUTH – the informal conversation that takes place about a product, problem or initiative.

10. AFTERWORD

The transition from the reckless giddiness of social media "gurus" to the strategic clarity of social communication is not done. The stakes are high – whether organisational communication recognises or ignores the fundamental freedom of choice that underpins participation in the workplace.

My belief in that fundamental freedom has brought me into contact with some awesome people, some of whom have had a lot to do with this book – chief among them my fellow COMMSCRUM agitators and co-founders of the 55-MINUTE GUIDE series, Kevin Keohane and Dan Gray, whom I met through the INTERNATIONAL ASSOCIATION OF BUSINESS COMMUNICATORS. This book (quite literally) could not have been published without them. I would also like to thank Kristen Sukalac and Barbara Govednik, the COUNCIL FOR COMMUNICATION MANAGEMENT, and my dad, former Wall Street Journal sport columnist Frederick C. Klein.

I owe a massive debt of gratitude to Mark Abernathy. Mark was my boss and surrogate parent in the early days of my political campaign career. Though my own political views drifted across the political aisle before I had the wisdom to leave politics (and the country) six years later, I've never forgotten the lessons he taught me.

Finally, I'm up for being social myself, and I welcome you to visit HTTP://SOCIALCOMMUNICATION55.WORDPRESS.COM to continue the conversation started here. In the meatime, here are some further resources you may find useful:

THE ART OF STRATEGY: A NEW TRANSLATION OF SUN ZU'S CLASSIC — R. L. WING

CHANGE 2.0: BEYOND ORGANISATIONAL TRANSFORMATION —
JOACHIM KLEWES & RALF LANGEN

MANAGING CHANGE — MAURY PEIPERL & TODD JICK

LINCHPIN: ARE YOU INDISPENSABLE? — SETH GODIN

THE REVOLUTION WILL NOT BE TELEVISED: DEMOCRACY, THE INTERNET AND THE OVERTHROW OF EVERYTHING — JOE TRIPPI

RULES FOR RADICALS — SAUL ALINSKY

THE STARFISH AND THE SPIDER: THE UNSTOPPABLE POWER OF LEADERLESS ORGANIZATIONS — ORI BRAFMAN & ROD A. BECKSTROM

THREE LAWS OF PERFORMANCE — STEVE ZAFFRON & DAVE LOGAN

THE TIPPING POINT — MALCOLM GLADWELL

TRIBAL LEADERSHIP: LEVERAGING NATURAL GROUPS TO BUILD A THRIVING ORGANIZATION — DAVE LOGAN, JOHN KING & HALEE FISCHER-WRIGHT

TRIBES: WE NEED YOU TO LEAD US — SETH GODIN

COMMSCRUM — WWW.COMMSCRUM.COM

COUNCIL FOR COMMUNICATION MANAGEMENT — WWW.CCMCONNECTION.COM

DIREKTZU/STRAIGHTTO — WWW.STRAIGHTTO.COM

EUROPEAN ASSOCIATION OF COMMUNICATION DIRECTORS — WWW.EACD-ONLINE.EU

INTERNATIONAL ASSOCIATION OF BUSINESS COMMUNICATORS — WWW.IABC.COM

ORGNET — WWW.ORGNET.COM

ABOUT THE AUTHOR

MIKE KLEIN is a member of the COMMSCRUM blogging ensemble and author of THE INTERSECTION, an occasional blog focusing on the connection between political, social, networked and corporate communication (http://intersectionblog.wordpress.com). He has a small private consulting practice and is currently based in Copenhagen, where he's addressing the challenge of introducing social communication principles into a traditional comms environment at a major oil company.

His other corporate communication roles included the merger of easyJet and Go Airlines in the UK, the UK launch of Digital Cable Television, and two efforts with US-based organisations which yielded Dilbertesque levels of frustration, but also enough blinding insights with which to move into the realm of authorship.

Prior to getting involved with corporate internal communications in 1997, while an MBA student at London Business School, Mike managed political campaigns for a variety of legislative, judicial and referendum campaigns throughout the Southern and Western United States. He is also former communication director of the National Jewish Democratic Council in the United States.

Mike is a member of the European Association of Communication Directors, the International Association of Business Communicators, and the Council of Communications Management, a leading US-based organisation of strategic corporate communicators. Mike is also a militant supporter of Tottenham Hotspur Football Club, a graduate of London Business School and the University of Wisconsin, an active member of Democrats Abroad and a holder of US and British Passports.

Far too many business books start with the false premise that offering meaningful insight requires exhaustive detail. They demand a huge investment from readers to wade through all the information provided and draw out what is relevant to them.

In a rapidly changing, time-starved world, it's an approach that's getting wronger and wronger. What CEOs and other busy business people desperately need is high-level strategic insight delivered in quick, simple, easy-to-digest packages.

Co-created by DAN GRAY and KEVIN KEOHANE, that's exactly what the 55-MINUTE GUIDES are designed to do. Instead of some 300-page pseudo-academic tome, they offer fresh perspectives and "must knows" on important topics that can be read from cover to cover in the course of a single morning's commute or a short plane ride.

In short, they are the antidote to most business books. A QUICK READ, not a long slog. Focused on BIG IDEAS, not technical detail. Promoting JOINED-UP THINKING, not functional bias. Written to EMPOWER THE READER, not to make the author look clever.

They're guided by the simple principle that INSIGHT GAINED PER MINUTE SPENT READING should be as high as possible. No fluff. No filler. No jargon. Just the things you REALLY need to know, written in plain English with clear and simple illustrations.

Lightning Source UK Ltd.
Milton Keynes UK
UKOW04f0157170114

224732UK00003B/120/P